About the author

At her family's request, Anne Bolam (née Peterkin), has written a synopsis of her time as a nurse, which is written in this book. She started writing it in 2016 but, due to her husband being seriously ill, picked up the cudgels again and finished the book in 2019, at the age of eighty-one. She is still as active as she can be, but for the time being has given up swimming and different pursuits. She plays the piano in an old folks' home and for the hymns in church when needed. She considers it good exercise for her right hand, which was affected by a stroke.

The advice she was given was: do the things you are able to do and forget about what you were able to do in the past. A wonderful piece of advice to try and follow.

DON'T DROP IT NURSE

ANNE M.G. BOLAM

DON'T DROP IT NURSE

Vanguard Press

VANGUARD PAPERBACK

© Copyright 2020
Anne M.G. Bolam

The right of Anne M.G. Bolam to be identified as author of
this work has been asserted by her in accordance with the
Copyright, Designs and Patents Act 1988.

All Rights Reserved

No reproduction, copy or transmission of this publication
may be made without written permission.
No paragraph of this publication may be reproduced,
copied or transmitted save with the written permission of the
publisher, or in accordance with the provisions
of the Copyright Act 1956 (as amended).

Any person who commits any unauthorised act in relation to
this publication may be liable to criminal
prosecution and civil claims for damages.

A CIP catalogue record for this title is
available from the British Library.

ISBN 978 1 784658 48 9

*Vanguard Press is an imprint of
Pegasus Elliot MacKenzie Publishers Ltd.*
www.pegasuspublishers.com

First Published in 2020

**Vanguard Press
Sheraton House Castle Park
Cambridge England**

Printed & Bound in Great Britain

Dedication

I dedicate this book to my dear husband, David,
who was one of the most tolerant of men. Also to
my daughters, Rosemary and Frances; their
husbands, Ken and Rory; and all four of my
fabulous grandchildren, Bethany, Naomi,
Charlotte and Michael.

I have donated letters and cine film from my time
in Aden to the Imperial War Museum.

Preface

Don't Drop It Nurse!

These words have been reverberating with me through the decades. As a young twenty-one-year-old nurse, I was specialling a patient on the kidney unit at the Edinburgh Royal Infirmary during its pioneering days in the 1960s.

The ward sister came in and said, "Staff Nurse Peterkin, you're not busy at the moment. I want you to go along to Theatre One to collect something there and take it straight away to Theatre Two."

I went tentatively along to Theatre One and was handed two stainless steel kidney dishes, one on top of the other. I was absolutely petrified as I thought I might slip on the shiny floor. I handed the dishes in to Theatre Two and it wasn't until a few days later that I realised that this was the first kidney transplant in the world. They were twin men in their fifties living in Edinburgh and one brother had given the other a kidney. History was made and I feel very proud to have been a part of it, although I was not present at the operation.

Chapter One
Early Childhood Memories

These words have been echoing in my mind for several decades, since I was a twenty-one-year-old staff nurse working at the Royal Infirmary, Edinburgh in 1960.

My family and friends have persuaded me to put my experiences into a book for posterity.

I was born in Edinburgh on 15th June 1938 to Dr and Mrs Grant Peterkin. My father was orphaned at the age of seventeen, his parents dying within three months of each other. He was determined to be a doctor and, because there were no student grants in those days, he had to raise the money himself, taking any lowly job he could and living in grotty digs. He met my mother at a dance and, at a later meeting at the dance hall said to my mother, "Thank goodness you are here. I don't need to make polite conversation." My mother was the fourth child of a Church of Scotland Minister and studied music, gaining a LRAM (Licentiate of the Royal Academy of Music).

Three years after they became engaged, they got

married, in 1935. They were hoping to start a family but sadly lost three babies. Mother became pregnant again and was advised to stay in bed so that she could carry her baby to term. When she was six months pregnant, feeling like an elephant lying in bed, friends came in and asked what my father was going to give her for Christmas. He announced, "A steriliser." This caused great mirth. As my parents were not financially well-off, they bought equipment for Dad's surgery as presents for each other.

I was born at 11 Randolph Crescent, Edinburgh, weighing seven and a half pounds.

In September 1939, when I was fifteen months old, the war started. Things were to change dramatically for everyone in Britain. My sister, Alison, was born on 31st July 1940, followed by my brother, William, on 8th July 1942.

My father was posted to North Africa and Italy in the RAMC, with the Eighth Army.

Fortunately, my grandmother lived about six miles away in Colinton. She had an Anderson shelter in the garden so that if a bomb dropped, we could run for shelter. We were issued with gas marks – Mickey Mouse masks. An advantage of being near Granny was that we had cousins to play with, as two of my aunts were living at *Ardkeen* (Granny's house) while their husbands were serving in the Forces.

During the war, we moved to the outskirts of Edinburgh, as our centrally placed flat became a risky place for children. My two-year-old sister was found walking around the edge of the basement after the railings had been removed to go towards building ships. Our new home had a lovely garden with a sandpit and Mother started to keep hens to supplement our diet. The eggs were preserved in Waterglass and we occasionally ate a hen.

We had to go to Redford Barracks to collect our rations of rose hip syrup and orange juice, to keep us healthy.

I remember my dad coming home on leave and taking me down to look at the Forth Bridge, where there were several barrage balloons. I asked my Dad why no one was playing with the lovely balloons.

Chapter Two
Childhood Memories of World War II

I was fifteen months old when the war started. My father had joined the Eighth Army as a dermatologist and syphilologist, as VD was rife among the Forces personnel. He had wanted to be a surgeon, but had fractured the scaphoid bone in his wrist while falling down Loch Nagar on King George V's estate, so had to move to another branch of medicine.

Dad was a medical office in the RAMC (Eighth Army) and was posted to North Africa and Italy, where he was in charge of a field hospital. As a result of this, he had an audience with Pope Pius XII. He wrote home to my mother to tell her that the pope had given a blessing to her and their three children. As she was the daughter of a Church of Scotland minister, she replied, "A fat lot of good that did; the children have all gone down with measles."

As the war progressed, my mother was very busy looking after me, my sister and my brother. My primary school was evacuated to the Scottish Borders, near

Selkirk. I was only four years old. I loved my school and, when Dad came home on leave to take me out, I did not want to go with him as I did not recognise this stranger in uniform.

Halcyon days suddenly came to an end for me as I developed acute earache and returned to Edinburgh to have double mastoid operations. I was in a children's nursing home for ten weeks (no NHS in those days). Parents were not permitted to visit very ill children, which was very sad and cruel for both parent and child. I remember hearing my mother's voice and ran out into the street to find her. At that time, a platoon of soldiers was marching past and one kindly chap scooped me up and returned me to the nursing home.

The very same day that I was discharged, my sister complained of severe tummy ache and was admitted to the bed I had vacated, and had her appendix removed. My poor mum. My baby brother at the age of six weeks had pneumonia during this time and nearly died.

I do believe that my experience as a patient and visiting my dad's department in the Royal Infirmary at Christmas sowed the seeds of my desire to be a nurse.

Life moved on and I went to St George's School for girls. My dad was discharged from the Army when I was about seven years old and I remember boasting to my school mates that I would have a "black daddy" as he had been in Africa. I was so disappointed when a white daddy appeared, bearing a large box of liquorice allsorts. (I suppose most of them were black.)

It was lovely having a daddy who had returned from the war, but my young brother took exception to this, as he had been told that the last time dad had home leave, that he had to look after his mum and sisters as he was now "the man of the house." Bill became very naughty, throwing shoes downstairs and, at the age of three, shouting, "I'm the king of the castle." He refused to pick up the shoes which resulted, after several warnings, that if he did not do as he was told he would have a smacked bottom. A rolled up British Medical Journal was the means by which this punishment was meted out, as my sister and I had learned to our cost, if we misbehaved while Dad was absent. It never did us any harm, but kept us in order.

Chapter Three
Secondary School and Teenage Years

I entered St George's School for girls at the age of seven. My mother was educated there along with her four sisters, so it was thought that the family tradition should be kept. My sister joined me two years later. All my aunts were very musical, each playing different instruments. If I recall, they could also all play the piano. My mother's chosen career was music and she gained an LRAM in London. She was a beautiful pianist and organist, but because my parents were hard up after the war, she became my father's unpaid secretary to enable him to set up his medical practice in Edinburgh.

I did not like school and was bullied. Being a sensitive child, I was frightened to stick up for myself. I was classed as a delicate child, as the result of my mastoid operations which led to a lot of time being absent from school. Fortunately, I was prescribed a sulphonamide drug, which saved my life. Antibiotics were in their infancy then.

I did enjoy music, tennis and lacrosse, and played

the piano at the junior version of the Edinburgh Festival in the Assembly Rooms, and sang with the school choir at the festival. I was chosen to sing with the choir when the Queen made her first visit to Edinburgh after her coronation.

From the age of four, I had become determined to be a nurse, so at the age of sixteen, my parents agreed that I should leave school and attend a local crammer college to try and obtain the necessary O Levels for admission to a nursing school. My head teacher had said that I was not bright enough and that I had had too much time off school to contemplate being a nurse. I was determined to prove her wrong.

I obtained the necessary three O Levels to apply and sallied forth to have an interview at the Princess Margaret Rose Hospital for crippled children. It was thought by my doctor that, in view of my medical history, I should start by nursing children, which would not be as heavy as nursing adults.

After a successful interview – the shortage of nurses at that time enabled me to secure a place with only three O Levels – I started my career, aged seventeen, on 29th February 1956.

We slept in very basic rooms in the nurses' home. Outside our rooms ran the fire escape, a good way to get in if we did not have a late pass. Those of us who had not gone out would go along the fire escape from room to room, hopping into the beds as the night sister shone her torch to make sure that we were all safe and sound. One girl got caught out, as she forgot to remove her hat.

Post-war, our food was still rationed and, once a week, butter and sugar were measured out to each individual.

We nurses started with a three month block of lectures and practical demonstrations, before we started our work on the wards. We had to learn how to give a bed bath, do dressings, learn anatomy, physiology and the general rules of working in a hospital.

I was assigned to Ward Two, to look after children up to five years old. Some of these poor wee souls had limbs in plaster, suffering from congenital dislocation of the hips, where they had to lie with their legs in the air, tied to a bar to maintain traction. Still's disease (children's arthritis) was quite common in those days. The little ones were wrapped in blankets to try and sweat out the disease. They got so hot.

Night duty was quite scary, as there lots of cockroaches scuttling down the corridor in front of us.

While I trained at this hospital, an adult wing was built, so the hospital became the Princess Margaret Rose Hospital, PMH. Unfortunately, the architect had not liaised with those who worked there and the doors to the bathrooms were not wide enough to accommodate wheelchairs etc. We had to put a plank on the patient's wheelchair and stretch it into the bathroom, sliding the patient on to another wheelchair to manage giving him or her a bath.

I was walking home from church with my mother one Sunday, when a gentleman asked how I liked working in the new wing. I commented that the architect should be sacked because of his lack of knowledge about disability. He was the culprit and apparently collapsed in church the following Sunday.

Prior to starting nursing, I became confirmed into our local Craiglockhart Church. I also sat my driving test, which I failed. I was scared in case I killed someone on the road or by my nursing ministrations and did not sleep well the night before. I was just seventeen when I sat my driving test, and I started my training the same day.

Christmas was a great time at the Princess Margaret Hospital as, of course, we gave the children as happy a time as we could. The consultants would come on to the wards and carve the turkeys. Father Christmas also came.

During the summer, the Edinburgh Military Tattoo came to the hospital grounds. Such excitement for the children and staff.

After two years at Princess Margaret Hospital, it was time to move on. I learned that I had done well in my exams and just missed an honours in orthopaedics by two marks, coming in the first two hundred candidates in Great Britain. So much for lack of academic ability to be a nurse.

Chapter four
Training at the Royal Infirmary, Edinburgh

On Friday 13th June (it is a good thing I am not suspicious), I arrived at the Royal Infirmary, Edinburgh to start my general training. Because I had spent two years of my training at the Princess Margaret Rose Orthopaedic Hospital, this knocked a year off my general training.

I was shown into a very old-fashioned building, the nurses' home, which had no heating in my bedroom, which was furnished with a bed, wardrobe, chair and dressing table. The woollen blanket I had on my bed was dated 1885. Things were made to last. The nurses had to use communal washing facilities. There was a common room with a coal fire in the grate.

We had a wake up call at 0630 hours and had to be in the dining room for tea and prayers at 0700 hours. I had an awful tussle each morning as I tried to make up my nurse's cap with all its pleats and pins. At that stage in our training we were called probationers.

My first ward was Ward Twelve, men's surgical, where even the doctors were frightened of the ward sister. I used to take the anaesthetist his coffee, which he took to the toilet with him to avoid the sister. Sister Blythe ran a well-disciplined ward and cared deeply for her patients. The other member of staff on the ward to be wary of was the domestic, who had been there for years and knew every nook and cranny on the ward. Woe betide any nurse if there was a spillage that was not wiped up immediately. It was good to get on the right side of her.

At 0845, the first shift of nurses went to have an enormous cooked breakfast, make their beds and tidy their rooms. The second shift went at 0930 hours. Bedrooms were inspected by home sister and punishment meted out if we were not up to standard.

Shifts through the hospital were as follows. On duty 0730 to 1400 hours, 1400 hours to 2130 hours. We might have a split shift from 1400 hours to 1700 hours, finishing at 2130 hours.

My next ward was Ward Twenty-Four, female medical, run smoothly by Sister Tait. It was a ward that catered for diabetic patients under the care of Sir Derek Dunlop. Sister asked a student nurse to give a patient with a heart condition an air-ring (meaning a rubber ring to sit on).

There was no sign of the patient and she found her sitting on the veranda in freezing weather, having an airing. She survived.

We had an excellent, tough training, working in many departments. I was nicknamed Salome when I worked in the operating theatre, as I was the skivvy chosen to dispose of limbs or any other bits that were removed from patients.

One of the wards I recall well was a male medical ward, run by a very strict Irish sister, Sister Mansfield. She was very anti-Christian. Other wards would normally allow groups to come and take services on the wards on Sundays. Not Sister Mansfield. When she was on holiday, a lovely Christian staff nurse was approached by a mission group, who asked if they could hold a service. The junior staff nurse agreed with her that it would be a good thing to try and cheer up the patients, as we had had four deaths in as many days.

The first hymn was announced, *The Sands of Time are Sinking Fast*, followed by a prayer, "We will now pray for those who have gone and those who are about to go."

Staff Nurse Hamilton and I were shocked at the insensitivity. She went to the leader and asked if they could please sing *Onward Christian Soldiers*, while I grabbed two boxes of tissues and started to comfort the patients.

After nurses obtained their RGN (Registered General Nurse) qualification, we were encouraged to work in speciality wards as staff nurses, deputising for the ward sisters when they were on holiday.

I had an interesting time working in the skin department (dermatology ward) and was elected to work on night duty, as my father was one of the chiefs (consultants) and it was thought better that we did not meet when on duty. Undeterred, I realised that some of our patients read daily papers with risqué cartoons in them. I would cut them out and plant them in my father's white coat, where he would find them in his pocket when he stopped for coffee. Apparently this gave him and his colleagues a morning laugh.

ENT (ear, nose and throat) was another memorable ward. Sister slept above the ward and, lo and behold, if a bell was not answered properly, she would be downstairs in her dressing gown to sort out the problem.

The ENT building was shared with the ophthalmic ward. I recall seeing a Russian lady of one-hundred-years-old having a cataract operation. In those days, patients had to spend ten days post-op blindfolded and in bed, having to use bedpans.

One night, I was crossing from the ENT building to join my friends for supper in the main hospital building. It was snowing and I was running late. All of a sudden, out of the dark, came a porter pushing a *barra for the bods*, a mortuary trolley. This was a hand-pushed trolley covered in a green canvas, laced up like a tent top. This very short porter, who had a limp, started pushing the vehicle up the hill to the morgue, but he slipped and fell backwards, and the body shot out into the snow. I went over to pick up the corpse, with the porter chastising him for not taking the trolley via the warm corridors instead of taking a short cut.

I promised him that I would not give away his experience, otherwise he would probably have lost his job. Needless to say, I went for my supper not feeling at all hungry and my colleagues exclaimed, "You are so pale, Anne, you look as if you have seen a ghost." Little did they know.

After a year as a staff nurse, we earned our Pelican Badge, which we wore with pride. I recall Night Sister Wilson looked very fed up, as she had lost her badge. It had fallen to the bottom of the Mediterranean when her ship was torpedoed during the war. She applied for another badge from the Nurse's League and received a letter which said, "You can have one this time, Nurse, but don't be so careless next time."

We were very fortunate to train at the Royal Infirmary, Edinburgh, as we gained a great deal of experience. So much pioneering was done in my time there.

Chapter five
Don't Drop It, Nurse

I was working in the dialysis unit at the Royal Infirmary, Edinburgh, nursing a pregnant lady suffering from pre-eclampsia toxaemia, when my ward sister came and said, "Nurse Peterkin, you are not busy at present, could you please go along to Theatre One and fetch something to take to Theatre Two.

I sped up to the theatre unit to Theatre One and was handed two stainless steel kidney dishes, one on top of the other, with the sister saying, "Go to Theatre Two as quickly as you can, and don't you dare drop it, Nurse."

I quickly glanced along the corridor at the shiny floor, praying that I would not slip, and handed the precious cargo safely into the hands of the sister.

It was not until a few days later that I learned that I was carrying the kidney that was used in the first transplant in the world. The operation was carried out on twin brothers in their fifties. It was a great success.

A reporter from the Daily Express phoned and offered the ward sister £200 to give them the personal details of the family. She refused but, sadly, a porter who had debts gave the game away and was sacked.

I believe this incident may have started cheque book journalism, as we know it today.

I feel very privileged to have taken part in pioneering medical history in 1960.

The words, "Don't drop it, nurse," still echo down the decades, especially if I am carrying something fragile.

Chapter six
Midwifery and More Orthopaedics

Having finished my training and gained my precious Pelican Badge, I decided that I would like to do a midwifery course, the reason being that if I should be travelling by train and a lady went into labour, should anyone discover that I was a trained nurse, they might call me into action. I thought that at least I should be prepared.

I was made welcome at the Nuffield Maternity Hospital. (This has now closed and midwifery care is now at the John Radcliffe Hospital.)

The Nuffield took in patients that were going to have difficult births. Sadly this was the era of thalidomide babies, where the mums had taken thalidomide (distaval) to prevent sickness in pregnancy. It was so sad to see these little infants with no legs or arms, but flipper-like appendages instead. Many of their faces were beautiful, with expressive eyes. I do believe that God had tried to compensate these children so that people would look into their faces instead of at their limbs. Some moved on to a rehabilitation unit called Chailey Heritage.

To become a full midwife, it was necessary to take parts one and two, part one in the hospital and part two 'on the district'. My application for part two had got mislaid by the authorities. However, I was not too dismayed as my first love was for orthopaedic nursing and I decided to apply to Wingfield Morris Orthopaedic Hospital for a job. (It is now the Nuffield Orthopaedic Hospital.)

I was interviewed by the severe looking matron and appointed as charge nurse of Nani Ward, the children's ward at that time. I was greeted by sister, who said that she was glad that I had come as she was about to go on holiday the next day and, as part of the ward was being decorated, she would be glad to miss this event. Most of the ward had been decorated, apart from a side ward called the Cardinal Room, as it had a picture of cardinals on the wall.

The decorating of Nani Ward was completed whilst I was there. I did mistake the chief anaesthetist for the plumber when he came into the ward wearing a pink towel around his neck. Theatre used to get very hot, so he needed some sort of mop, I suppose.

I was then moved as a charge nurse to Gibson Ward, which looked after adult female patients. My colleague, Wendy Holder, looked after Randle, the male ward. There were no ward sisters on the wards at that time because one was overseas and the other on long-term sick leave, so we got lots of experience.

When the sisters were due to return, it was time for me to move on. I was offered a night sister's post, but nights had never suited me and, at the age of twenty-four, I felt I was a bit young to be tied down and that I ought to see a bit of the world.

Chapter seven
Princess Mary's Royal Air Force Nursing Service

I returned to Edinburgh, living with my parents and working as a junior sister at the Officers' Association Nursing Home, Belgrave Crescent. This was very convenient, as it was the house next door to that of my parents. It was also called the Gun Club, as the matron was called Miss Gunn. She was full of fun and not at all strict.

I applied to join the PMRAFNS (Princess Mary's Royal Air Force Nursing Service) and had the interview in London. Much to my delight, I was accepted, with a starting date of December 1964.

This was an exciting time and I had to go to Boyd Cooper in London to be kitted out with the various forms of uniform it was mandatory to wear.

I was posted to RAF Hospital Halton with the other new recruits. This was in order to have lectures and do the 'square bashing'. It was snowing when we arrived and I remember losing a contact lens in the snow. Some very helpful young RAF men helped me to find it.

The Sisters' Mess was very cosy. We each had our own room and soon made friends.

During the week we went to lectures and at the weekend we were appointed to wards. Mine was the male orthopaedic ward, with Squadron Officer Singer in charge. She was delighted to see me as she was going off for the weekend. There was I, left in charge, once again not knowing the patients or the ward routine.

The commanding officer was due to do an inspection the following Monday and sister wanted everything just right. I was detailed to give LAC Saunders the job of Cardinal Polishing the lavatories. I had never heard of this stuff before and said, "Make sure the seats are nice and shiny." It was supposed to have gone on the floor and apparently the laundry were very puzzled as to why the men's pyjama trousers were red.

First Posting: RAF Hospital Ely

After the statutory time at Halton, it was time to move on. I was posted to RAF Hospital Ely along with Heather Naylor (née Grant), with whom I have been friends ever since.

This hospital is set in the Fens and at that time took a great many NHS patients from Addenbrookes Hospital, Cambridge. This gave us enormous experience, as I nursed two patients in oxygen tents, something I had not experienced before, and also relieved the NHS waiting list.

Once again, I was delighted to work on the orthopaedic ward. There was a lad from Ely, called Brian, who came in unconscious with multiple fractures. He was eighteen and had come off his motorbike. Brian had been unconscious for several weeks and, during the consultants' ward round, unbeknown to me, started undoing the pearl buttons I had at the front of my uniform. He was heard to say, "Ain't you the little bit what works in the Co-Op?" The doctors and their entourage thoughts this was hilarious.

Brian did recover, although he was left with a bad limp, but in his own words, "Sister, it is good to be back pulling the birds." He came back to see me bearing an enormous box of chocolates.

RAF Hospital Khormaksar Beach, Aden

The time came for us nursing sisters to be posted abroad. My posting was to Aden, and our mess dress for posh functions was very elaborate, with gold epaulettes and buttons.

I felt very excited as I boarded the Britannia plane at Gatwick, along with other military personnel and some families.

After about half an hour in the air, the pilot announced that there was trouble with the engine and he was going to abort the fuel over the channel and return to Gatwick. What a disappointment! The airline put us up at the Grand Hotel, Brighton, and I can recall having a lovely single en-suite bedroom and phoning my parents, who naturally thought I was phoning from Aden.

After a long twenty-three hour flight, with a stop in Bahrain, we landed at RAF Khormaksar and were taken to the hospital. To my amazement, there was a camel guard at the entrance. The men wore very colourful outfits. The hospital was celebrating its Christmas party, to which I was invited. I did feel a bit jet lagged, but felt that I should join as we were given the following day off to adjust to the heat and do the usual admin on arrival.

I was glad to get to my air-conditioned room eventually. At that time, there were eight of us nursing at the hospital.

We initially looked after soldiers and families of the APL (Arab Protectorate Levi). There was a male ward and a female ward, separated by the sandy desert and a rough path that the theatre trolley used to wobble up and down on.

We sisters had our own block and the male doctors lived in the Officers' Mess, which we shared for meals and recreation. There were two surgeons, one anaesthetist and two physicians when we first arrived. Our matron, Doreen Francis, was a cheerful, caring lady who was a wonderful support to her young sisters. She had a great deal of responsibility as the British were gradually pulling out of Aden. We had a wonderful Maltese chef who provided us with very imaginative menus.

Chapter eight
Nursing in Aden

The hours we worked were designed to help us cope with the heat. Half a day was considered quite long enough for us girls. We started work at 0700 hours and finished at 1300 hours, then worked from 1300 hours until about 2100 hours, when the night staff took over.

Our off duty was mainly spent at Tarshyne Beach, about eight miles from the hospital. The local bus went all the way. We had a wonderful plethora of chaps willing to chat us up. An ice cream stall was conveniently placed at the back of the beach. During the cool season, October to April, we were able to swim in the sea, but in the hot season there were shark nets to keep us safe. Swimming was not advised.

After my initiation into RAF life overseas, I was put on duty in the female Arab ward. This I found fascinating. The children were all put in with the mums who, of course, had to rest. I made a children's ward, which was a great success. The women had never had proper sanitary protection and adjutant drew my attention to the fact that behind the toilets there was a tree where the patients had thrown their sanitary towels out of the window. They landed on the tree, looking like Christmas decorations. Of course, I had to arrange for them to be removed.

A patient came in for a gall bladder operation. I asked an ayah (female care assistant) to give her an abdominal shave. I went to check the patient and found that she had not had a shave. In fact, her sister had felt tired and had hopped into the bed, and she had the shave while the patient had gone for a wash.

Another ayah was asked to watch a patient who had a retained placenta after a delayed miscarriage. While I rang Doctor Hakim, she left the patient and informed me that she had done as they do on the *bundu*, tickled the lady's nose with a matchstick, and the placenta had come straight out. She has used a stick or piece of straw when necessary.

Medicine abroad certainly has its fascinations!

I was then put on duty on the male ward. A very rickety trolley took the patients over the sand to the operating theatre, which was quite near the men's ward. The men and women were kept apart because of purdah. As soon as a request for blood came through, all the visitors left the wards. It was a good way to get rid of unwanted folk.

Night duty then called me and I worked between both the Arab wards. We had a terrorist prisoner under guard on the men's ward. The PBX (telephone operator) informed that me Arab soldiers were coming some time during the night to remove the prisoner. I went to the duty officer's bedroom to inform him. British soldiers were informed and the prisoner was removed to a British Guard room. The enemy did come to take the prisoner and, as far as I know, the captive patient went peacefully.

One night I was called to the men's ward. One chap had a very high temperature. I recommended that he be given a tepid sponge, as I reckoned he had malaria. I found two of the carer soldiers throwing buckets of luke warm water over the poor fellow. His temperature certainly came down sharply. He was sitting on a red waterproof mattress.

Night duty could be frightening, as at that time I was on my own with the Somali ayahs and Arab soldiers for company. Wild dingo dogs patrolled the compound and it was a matter of listening for them to try and avoid them when traversing the compound.

The PBX was based in the centre of the compound and reasonably accessible if we needed him.

Chapter nine
Aden – Nursing in the European Wing

After a few months it was decided to build a European wing. The hospital at Steamer Point was getting inundated with casualties and there was room at Khormaksar Beach Hospital (KBH) for a helicopter landing strip. Steamer Point Hospital was the main general RAF hospital in Aden and had the usual amenities for RAF personnel and their families, but was becoming difficult to manage with the number of casualties that were being admitted.

I was moved to the new wing, where we had a super casualty department, theatres and four wards, plus an officers' ward. It was lovely to work in such a new place with air conditioning etc. There were also single rooms at the back.

Our staff consisted of Arab men who objected to cleaning the toilets that the British patients had used. We had two types of lemonade (too strong to dringk): 1) orange powder; and 2) lemon powder. I had a competition to see which side was the cleanest (left or right) and took the lavatory brushes, showing them what to do. We had such fun. The men were nursed by British Medical Orderlies.

The cases we nursed included: the usual gunshot wounds, grenade injuries, tanks being blown up etc; appendices; circumcisions; hernias; and surgical operations that might take place in any general hospital.

The entrance had a corporal keeping watch. Outside the A&E was the helicopter landing strip. If we were lucky, we would get a phone call about an impending admission. If not, a helicopter could be heard coming towards us.

The dust was awful, covering everything, personnel as well as furnishings. This was, of course, due to the sand.

We had many amusing incidents whilst working on the European wing. During all the business we had to make time for visitors of all shapes and sizes. Several senior officers' wives decided to pay us a call. The cleanliness of some of the lads left a lot to be desired, due to very basic washing facilities, which meant that they required circumcisions. One of the women said, "Which side did sister say you had your operation?" I hadn't said anything, but replied, "He's sitting on it, ma'am." There was muffled laughter in the background.

One day I was walking past a patient's bed. His stitches burst. The anaesthetist wrote in his notes that I had walked past and wiggled my hips at his bedside. I forbade him to read *Playboy* magazine while he was convalescing.

One day we were expecting a special visitor in the ward. It turned out to be the Bishop of Sudan. I had a young lad in with a fractured spine, who said he could not believe in the virgin birth. I discreetly introduced the bishop to him and he sat down beside him, gently explaining the mystery. The other lads were agog with interest. A visit worth recalling.

At one time, I was on night duty with two young Irish RAF orderlies. They informed me that Gunner Wilks was moaning because he was going to Blighty on the casevac the next day and had not even touched an Arab woman. I said that I could sort this out and went over to the female Arab wing and borrowed a purdah (whoo, did it smell!). Gunner Wilks took ages to come, while I waited patiently in the corridor for him to come and caress my arm. He had waited for the kettle to boil so that he could have a shave. At the end of that time there was an SOS, which meant there was a helicopter on its way with a casualty. As I was in charge of the ward, I had to swiftly change and get ready for action. Never a dull moment!

At Christmas time, several of the lads got very homesick, so I purchased pipe cleaners, crepe paper and borrowed sheets from the ward. We made a wonderful ski scene which I captured on cine film. It gave the lads and myself something to focus on.

My patients on the European wing were a very mixed bag, as you can imagine. There were RAF orderlies doing the nursing and Arab sweepers carrying out the domestic work. I could not understand why the toilet basins kept breaking, but realised that the Arabs stood on them to use them as their own toilets were holes in the ground. The British boys refused to clean them until I explained they were the ones who were supposed to use them and gave them the coloured lemonade powder competition.

At the time I was there, 1964 to 1966, the British were pulling out of Aden. I have taken some cine film of CO Mad Mitch sorting the enemy in Crater.

The Arabs were petrified of the Cameronians, who they nicknamed the 'Poisoned Dwarves'. I nursed men from all the regiments, plus RAF and Navy personnel.

I can vividly remember an eighteen-year-old marine from Edinburgh. You could have got a lady's handbag into his abdomen, where a grenade had landed. His parents were sent for and I spent some time with him and them, discussing Edinburgh, my childhood home. He died in my arms. I was so glad to have been able to offer some comfort.

I remember a twenty-one-year-old trooper who got the Commanding Officer's commendation for saving his officer from his tank, which caught fire. The trooper had massive burns all over his body and, due to having been up country, where there were no women, he thought I was an angel with my white cap on. I was his 'special nurse'.

One of my fellows was a twenty-five-year-old sergeant, who could not sleep, in spite of medication plus plus. He was in a ward with his injured men. I thought that, had I been him, I would have howled and wanted to kick the place down. I took him into my office and suggested that he have a single room for the night, and that only he and I knew he had to be left alone. He spent the night venting his anger and bereavement, then slept like a baby. He had no problems sleeping after that. I feel he had PTSD. I had a lovely postacard from Blighty.

At about this time, we obtained a purpose built prison ward, where the enemy were incarcerated. It was under the charge of the British, although we nursing sisters had keys. It was quite a palaver giving the inmates their drugs etc and making sure that they did not escape.

Chapter ten
Holidays

While in Aden, we were allowed to spend two weeks in Kenya. This was fantastic, as the hotel we stayed in was the Norfolk Hotel. I can still remember the colours and scents of the bougainvillea which seemed to invade each part of Nairobi.

Heather and Clive became engaged in Nairobi, so there was great excitement. (Heather was a close friend and Clive worked in the transport and equipment branch of the RAF. David, who served as a dental officer in the RAF, and I met them at an interdenominational Christian Union in Aden.) During the visit, trips to the game park were organised and we shared a minibus with several Army officers. I recall being chased by an elephant. What a thrill!

I had two trips. During the second one, I stayed with my sister in Machakos, where she was teaching. David came and joined me. My sister and I had the thrill of travelling to Malindi, north of Mombasa, where we went with a young man and travelled along the rickety road in his car. We stayed on the way in dwellings attached to safari parks. Most of them appeared to have swimming pools, which was fantastic. Also, we enjoyed views of the animals coming down to the water holes at night. At Malindi, we slept in basic wooden tents.

On my way back from Kenya to Aden, I travelled by Hastings Aircraft, the only girl aboard. The crew let me pilot her home and I followed the wrong river in Ethiopia. What a laugh.

We service personnel were also allowed two weeks in Blighty. I had a lovely time with my Scottish parents and family in the Scottish Highlands, where it was so warm I only wore a blouse, cardigan and skirt. Happy memories in October!

Chapter eleven
Aden – Continuing Adventures and Music

As well as being very involved with St Andrew's church, I belonged to the Aden Light Operatic Society (ALOS), which consisted of service personnel and civilians. At first I acted as props, as I was too late to take a part in *The Pirates of Penzance* by Gilbert and Sullivan, having arrived in Aden after the rehearsals had started. Everyone was very friendly and we subsequently put on *The White Horse Inn*, *The Mikado* and *La Belle Helene* by Offenbach. We had a wardrobe of clothes for acting and some of the ladies were very handy with a needle.

I used to give a car-load of teachers a lift to the rehearsals. One of them told me that she was madly in love with David. She was a patient of his and very scraggy, poor soul. I knew her and called her 'the Sparrow'. His sergeant said, "I've seen better, sir." One afternoon, David and I had arranged to meet on the beach. The Sparrow raced on ahead and said hello to him, not realising that we were an item. Poor soul, I felt so sorry for her. I continued to give lifts to the teacher.

Jack Reilly was the conductor of ALOS. He and his wife, Brenda, were very hospitable and, much of the time, those of us in the singing group enjoyed meals and parties in their home. I believe that Jack's career was in music in the Army.

I am sorry that I did not keep in touch with the Reillys after they left Aden.

Due to the security situation, ALOS was a wonderful distraction for service and civilian personnel. Rehearsals were held at RAF Khormaksar, so we were well guarded.

I remember going to the cinema, which was in the open air. There were soldiers standing guard above us, making sure we were safe. We saw *The Sound of Music*, a wonderful film.

Chapter twelve
Aden, Off Duty

We sisters had a marvellous time off duty. There were reputed to be five hundred men to each woman. Many of the men were married and some were too young for us. I was very attached to my little church, PMUB (Presbyterian Methodist United Board) it was called then. I was very blessed and had two superb padres in post there.

I used to help run the children's six to twelve-year-olds on a Monday afternoon. I ran this with two RAF chaps who, at times, were on guard duty. One afternoon, I arrived at RAF Khormaksar to find that both chaps had been called for duty. I was left with thirty children on my own. One lad persisted in chucking darts at the other children. I said that if he did not stop, I would put him in the porch for the safety of everyone. I put him in the porch and promptly forgot about him. That evening, the padre caught me after the evening service. I thought he was going to tick me off, but no, he had no one to play for the service that evening, so much to his surprise, I swiftly agreed. Matron Doreen Francis attended that service and was delighted to let me have time off duty.

While I worshipped at the church, sadly a young lad committed suicide. Consequently, an aviary was built and a coffee shop. We had this and others deaths in mind when we built it. There was so little for the lads to do out there. It was good to get involved with the running of the place. We also held a sports day, involving as many people as possible.

The church became quite a centre.

Off duty, four of us became very involved with the Officers' Christian Union. We met for Bible study every week in a different home. This could be a member of any of the three services. I became very friendly to David. My friend, Heather, became friendly with Clive Naylor. We were all married for fifty years and were godparents to each other's elder daughter.

Out of twelve sisters serving at the same time as me, eight got married. Poor matron, what a gang we were!

Chapter thirteen
Animals – from Childhood to Blighty

Throughout my life, I have always enjoyed the company of animals. As a child, we had a selection of dogs, ranging from a Scottie to a labrador.

My children had a garden where rabbits and guinea pigs were encouraged, plus their babies.

When nursing on the district, I did enjoy helping with Riding for the Disabled, until I had my back injury. This was on a Thursday, on my half day.

David and I had several dogs during our long married life. The last one was a sprollie – part border collie, part springer spaniel. He had to be put to sleep five weeks before David died. He was called Lucky. He was such good company and a wonderful support to us. I missed my dogs when nursing away from home and throughout my life I have always appreciated animals.

Chapter fourteen
Blighty and Homecoming

At last, I was told I would be going home in September. Unfortunately, I contracted infective hepatitis, probably from a Somali lady who kept vomiting. I certainly went yellow and the lads on my ward played *The Yellow Submarine* for me. I was admitted to Steamer Point Hospital as a patient. I took my cine camera in with me and was able to film the Post Office being blown up by the terrorists and the ambulances rushing to hospital.

It was advised that I would go home as a medical case by casevac, but I felt I had not finished my tour, so went back on duty until it was officially time to leave.

What a marvellous homecoming I had. David met me at Gatwick Airport, with Clive meeting Heather. It was about 0300 hours. I spent the night with David's parents in Guildford before travelling to Edinburgh to meet my family.

I was based at RAF Wroughton hospital, where I had planned to do the aeromedical training with a view to working in Kenya with the Flying Doctor.

In March 1967, David and I had a holiday on the Settle to Carlisle Railway Line and got engaged at Horton in Ribblesdale. We bought my lovely golden sapphire engagement ring in Skipton. On 21st October that year we got married. David left the RAF in December 1967 when we were living in Thirsk, David being based at RAF Topcliffe.

We lived with David's parents for eight weeks while David took up a post in Reading with the Community Dental Service. I found a bungalow to rent and obtained a position as a district nurse, wanting to find a good GP so that we could start a family. We found an excellent GP in Pangbourne, Dr Alan Stroud, who, with his wife, became a family friend.

I worked as a district nurse until I became pregnant with my lovely daughter, Rosemary. When she was eight months old, I got glandular fever and it was thought that I might not conceive again. However, with help from the drug, Clomid, and the John Radcliffe Hospital, Oxford, after nearly three years I found I was expecting again. Another daughter, Frances, was born in November 1973. Joy, oh joy.

In the meantime, I did some private nursing through Mrs Gardiner's Nursing Agency. When the girls were old enough, I was appointed as a bank district nurse.

They were at playgroup and school by then.

I had several adventures on the district. On a Sunday morning, when the surgeries were all closed, I had to go into a flat in bed and breakfast land. I was rather anxious as the flat seemed to be full of Irish men. I heard someone ask who was coming into the flat and, via the hatch, heard a voice ask about a shipment of arms coming in. The patient had a grazed leg and was reluctant to tell me how it had occurred. I was sure the house contained Irish terrorists and had decided to go in mufti on the bus the next day and report the incident to the police. The next morning, I turned on Meridian News to find a police raid had been carried out on the very flat I had been in. Arms were found in Hardwick Estate. I had stumbled on an IRA cell.

At one surgery where I worked, there had been a robbery and all the whooping cough vaccines had been nicked. We nurses had visions of the thieves going around Reading coughing.

When the girls were older, I decided that I would apply for a twenty hours a week job, and had been asked by the GPS to apply, as I had covered maternity leave and other absences in the district. I was told that I would have to do the district nurse course as I did not have the certificate to say District Nurse Trained – this after eight years in the job. I dutifully did a year on the course and ended up with a super job as the first district nurse at Burdwood surgery, Thatcham. We had wonderful fun, as I was with a bunch of four district nurses, all Christian, and we met for a pub lunch every month.

I was still working as a district nursing sister when an eighteen stone patient landed on me, and this put my back out. I had six months off and then chose to work as a school nurse for twenty hours a week.

My back became too painful to work and I was helping to care for my elderly in-laws, so decided to give up clinical nursing. It was like a bereavement.

The Royal College of Nursing found me a job with the Medical Advisory Service. This meant working from home on the telephone, covering the general line – insomnia and folk with various other problems.

Eventually, I started the nurse led medical helpline for the Foreign Office. Apparently a nurse was chosen because we let patients make their own decisions.

In the meantime, my daughters had each produced two children and my husband had a life-changing brain haemorrhage in 2012. It was decided that we would live near Fran and her family, as Rose had her in-laws living five miles away.

We moved to a lovely bungalow in Holmer Green. This was opposite the supportive Methodist church.

I had two back operations in Reading.

Unfortunately, they went wrong. David sadly developed a form of leukaemia and ended up nursing me when he was supposed to be going through a good patch. I latterly looked after him when he became seriously ill and consequently died. We had a wonderful service for him.

At present, I am living happily in a sheltered flat five minutes from the bungalow and, in spite of having a stroke as well as my back operations, am remarkably cheerful.

Chapter fifteen
Life in Blighty

David and I enjoyed living in the bungalow and getting involved in St Mary's Church, Purley on Thames. I played the organ for over forty years and was on the PCC and Mission Committee. David was also on the PCC and joined the Deanery Synod, where he enjoyed meeting folk from other churches. We held Bible studies in our home, where David was a leader.

We eventually moved to a four bedroomed house to cope with our expanding family, but stayed with St Mary's Church. A few years later, I was asked by the rector to be the organist at St Nicholas in Sulham. This I agreed to and I enjoyed playing for weddings, as well as Sunday services and, of course, the occasional funeral. We donated a bench for the churchyard to St Mary's, and a wintering flowering tree.

When Rose was just over a year old, I was walking her out of Hillview Close, our road, and was clobbered by a lady who wanted me to take her place on the Committee of Arthritis and Rheumatism. I agreed to this and was publicity officer for twenty-one years, then three years as chairman. I had nursed children with arthritis many years before and therefore had a special interest in the society.

Rose and Fran both went to Long Lane Primary School and then moved on to Denefield Secondary School. Rose excelled at music and Fran at sport.

I was appointed as a parent governor and served for seven years. At the end of that time, I was approached by an ex-military man in our church, who asked me if I would take his place on SSAFA (Soldiers, Sailors, Airforce Family Association). It was a privilege to serve ex-service folk and their families for twenty years. I was appointed a caseworker, then divisional secretary for Reading and district.

It was an interesting time, as the Ghurkas were brought to this country. We had to find them food, accommodation etc. They had no National Insurance, medical certificates etc. Many were staying in accommodation that would normally take two to four people, with ten packed in a single room.

There were men and women who served in the world wars who needed help – new cookers, fridges, help with benefits. Personnel in other conflicts were quite often affected. Holidays were sometimes offered.

Chapter sixteen
Happy Days Pre-retirement

Before David and I both retired, we decided to have some really interesting holidays as well as our trips on the Settle to Carlisle Railway Line.

In 1997, on our ruby wedding anniversary, we were invited to go to the Holy Land with our good friends, Heather and Clive Naylor. They, too, were celebrating their ruby wedding anniversary that year, as were a couple called Mary and Joseph. The family gave us a lovely party later that year, at the Six Bells, Beenham in Berkshire.

A few years later, we went to Greece and followed Saint Paul's journeys through Greece with Heather and Clive.

David and I, in between times, enjoyed trips with the small Majestic shipping line. This was on a converted Irish fishing boat. There is a fleet of three travelling up the west coast of Scotland. We enjoyed the experience so much that we went three times on the Glen Tarsan. We had a very comfy en-suite cabin with all mod cons. The food was Scottish, home grown or reared.

The first time I travelled, I had recently had a hip replaced. The consultant said that he was happy for me to go. I had a chat with the captain, stating that I would be quite happy staying on board and reading a book, letting my husband go on terra firma.

His reply was, "You saved my life in Aden, when I got blown up. I would recognise your face and your walk anywhere."

We called the captain Taffy. He had served with the Welsh Guards and the SAS. We had been in Aden at the same time. His face had been unrecognisable. I explained that I was part of a team that saved his life.

He and a colleague gently lifted me down to the tender and I was able to go on the land.

I have so many tales to recount about my nursing career and other experiences. It is difficult to know what to include and what to leave out.

Anne, aged eighteen

Anne, Khormaksar Beach, 1965

Arab sweeper, RAF Khormaksar, 1965

Khormaksar Beach, 1965, behind the hospital

Clive, Anne and David, Round Island Bay, Aden, 1965

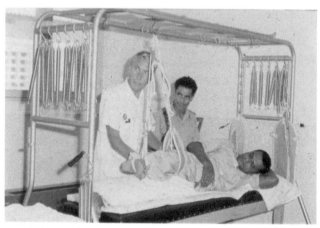

Khormaksar Beach Hospital, Arab ward, 1966

Tarshyne Beach, Aden, 1966

Anne, 1964-1967

Anne, engagement photo, March 1967
Belgrave Crescent Gardens, Edinburgh

Anne and David's wedding, with Clive (best man) and
Alison (bridesmaid)

Anne and David's wedding at the
Dean Parish Church, Edinburgh, 21st October 1967,
with Anne's sister, Alison

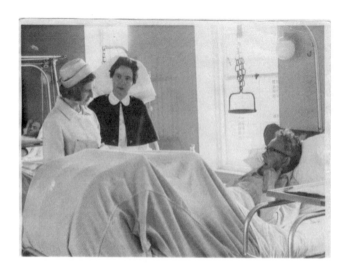

Anne with Princess Alexandra, RAF Hospital, 1967

St Mary's Church, Purley-on-Thames
Anne played the organ there for over forty years,
1968 to 2008

St Nicholas Church, Berkshire
Anne played the organ there for ten years

Anne with two grandchildren, 1999
Bethany, aged three and Naomi, eight weeks

Pangbourne and District Committee,
Gold Badge Award, April 1996

Lucky, July 2008

Anne and David, David's eightieth birthday, July 2016

Clive and Heather on their golden wedding
anniversary, January 1967 to January 2017

Glen Tarsan, Majestic Shipping Line

Anne Bolam, SSAFA Caseworker, 1994 to 2013

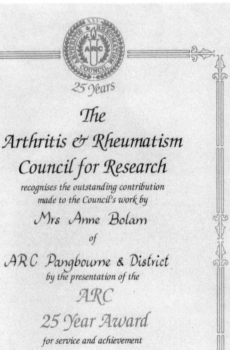

25 Years

The
Arthritis & Rheumatism
Council for Research

recognises the outstanding contribution
made to the Council's work by

Mrs Anne Bolam

of

ARC Pangbourne & District

by the presentation of the

ARC
25 Year Award

for service and achievement

_____
PRESIDENT

2·4·96
DATE

A Registered Charity No. 207711

THE ARTHRITIS AND RHEUMATISM COUNCIL

FOR RESEARCH IN GREAT BRITAIN AND THE COMMONWEALTH
Copman House, St Mary's Court, Chesterfield, Derbyshire S41 7TD
Telephone: 01 246 558 033 Fax: 01 246 558 007 Email: info@arc.org.uk

A Registered Charity

18th August 1997

Mrs. A. Bolam,
6, Hillview Close,
Tilehurst,
READING
RG31 6YX

Dear Anne,

I have just read your letter which arrived whilst I was away on
holiday. I am very sorry to learn that we are going to be losing you
at the end of the year but quite understand your reasons for needing
more time for other things.

I am very aware, Anne, of the amount of time and effort which you
have contributed to our cause so generously and I welcome this
opportunity to put on record our deep appreciation for all that you
have done for Arthritis Research.

With 26 years service to this Charity, you are thought of as a very
special friend and the Pangbourne Branch of ARC will miss you
greatly. However, I am relieved to hear that you will still help out
whenever possible - your skills and experience will not be lost to
us entirely!

We count ourselves lucky indeed to have been on the receiving end of
dedication such as yours: your stalwart support has been greatly
appreciated by the Regional Organisers you have assisted and by those
of us here at Head Office who know just how committed you have been
to our Charity and its aims.

Mere words are totally inadequate to express our gratitude to you
Anne. Thank you so very much indeed and our very best wishes for
good health and much happiness in the future.

With kind regards and best wishes.

Yours sincerely,

K. R. HAWES
Director,
Regional Organisation

Patron H.R.H. The Duchess of Kent.
President Dr D. Woods, DSO. Chairman of the Council Dr Robert Boyle FR. Chairman Executive Committee Professor J. Wright, MD DRCP, OMP Committee J Hunter, FCP MRCP.
Registered Charity No. 207711. A company limited by guarantee. A Public institution. Company no. 442770. Registered Office in England.

<u>Mrs Anne Bolam. Citation for SSAFA Meritorious Service Award.</u>

Anne Bolam was an outstanding success as Divisional Secretary for Reading Division. Thanks to her efforts the case numbers increased by 300% and the number of caseworkers more than doubled. Under Anne's leadership the division had very high morale and the office ran most efficiently.

Anne joined SSAFA FH in 1994 and took over as Division Secretary in Mid 2005. When she took over the division was short of caseworkers and short of cases. Prior to 2005 Anne was the Branch Publicity Officer as well as a caseworker in Reading. As Div Sec she has continued to carry out many cases each year. She handed over in Jan 2011 to hand over a going concern to a younger person and to spend more time with her family and grandchildren.

Anne has continued to serve SSAFA in West Berkshire Division by carrying out cases, as well as helping with publicity and fundraising.

Anne served as Flt Lt in PMRAFNS for 4 years, including in Aden, in the 1960's. She worked in Reading and West Berkshire as a District Nursing Sister and Community School Nurse for 15 years.

In addition to her work for SSAFA FH, Anne played the organ at St Mary's Church Purley-on-Thames from 1974 to 2011. She has also played the organ at St Nicholas, Sulham for 9 years and is currently a Church Warden.

Prior to 1994 Anne was chairman of Pangbourne Arthritis and Rheumatism Council. She was also a governor of Denefield school (11-18 years), Tilehurst, Reading.

Anne deserves recognition for all she has done for SSAFA FH in Reading and Berkshire.

ssafa

SSAFA
Queen Elizabeth House
4 St Dunstan's Hill
London EC3R 8AD

T 0845 130 0975
F 0207 403 8815
www.ssafa.org.uk

From: **General Sir Kevin O'Donoghue KCB CBE**
Chairman

Direct Line: 020 7463 9207
E-Mail: kevin.od@ssafa.org.uk
PA: 020 7463 9202
E-Mail: lorna.w@ssafa.org.uk

Mrs Anne Bolam
6 Hillview Close
Tilehurst
READING
RG30 6YX

26 September 2013

Dear Mrs Bolam

I have been advised that you have decided to retire after 19 years of dedicated volunteer service in our Berkshire Branch, and I write to send you good wishes for the future.

I know I speak for everyone, Branch and Central Office, when I say how very grateful we are for all that you have done for SSAFA over the years as a volunteer. I know you will be greatly missed.

It gives me great pleasure to send you this certificate, and it brings with it the thanks and best wishes of everyone here at Central Office.

Yours sincerely,

Kevin O'Donoghue

Lifelong support for our Forces and their families

The Soldiers, Sailors, Airmen and Families Association - Forces Help
Registered Charity No. 210760 (in England) and SC038056 (in Scotland).
Established 1885. Incorporated by Royal Charter.

Patron: HM The Queen
President: HRH Prince Michael of Kent GCVO
Chairman: General Sir Kevin O'Donoghue KCB CBE

 Lifelong support for our Forces and their families

Honorary Life Membership

of SSAFA

Berkshire Branch

is hereby conferred on

Mrs Anne Bolam

in grateful recognition of 20 years dedicated service in the interests of our Forces and their families

Signed *S Macfadyen*

Date *1 April 2014*

Branch President

Signed *MWH Robert*

Date *1 April 2014*

Branch Chairman

Patron HM The Queen
President HRH Prince Michael of Kent GCVO

Registered Charity No. 210760 Est. 1885 Registered Charity (Scotland) No. SC038056